Millionaire In the Making

A Handy Guide to Financial Health

Dedication

To Chaz and Saige my two children who are just
starting their adventure of adulthood.

Contents

Start where you are. Use what you have. Do what you can.

Arthur Ashe

Introduction

This book provides a guide to pre-teens, teens, young adults, and other individuals who are starting their journey of personal finance and wealth building.

The availability of vast amounts of information via the internet and resources such as books and articles, can cause information overload. The overwhelming effects of information overload can be intimidating and serve as a barrier in your journey toward financial health and wealth building.

Millionaire in the Making provides information in a simplified format that is useful and actionable. The book offers practical tips and pointers that you can systematically implement in your current situation to accomplish your financial goals.

Millionaire in the Making compiles intuitive information and strategies, which I hope will provide a roadmap to help you along the journey.

The book touches on all aspects of personal finance that are critical to your financial health. Each topic in the book gives pragmatic advice and insights that are easy to follow and implement. The information presented is detailed yet specific, so you can apply it pretty quickly to reach your personal finance goals.

One vital piece of advice I would like to impart to the reader is that your journey to financial health and wealth building can start at any age. Of course, starting sooner rather than later is ideal. But it's never too late to start. Start where you are, no matter how old you are or how much you earn.

What is Personal Finance?

Personal finance is the management of money and financial decisions made by individuals or households. It is important to understand personal finance to make informed decisions about saving, spending, and investing money.

Personal finance helps individuals achieve their financial goals and provides financial security for the future.

Importance of personal finance

Personal finance comprises investing, saving, and creating a budget.

Making wise financial decisions and reaching financial objectives require an understanding of personal finance.
The process of financial planning includes tracking spending to make smart future financial plans, developing a budget, setting objectives, coming up with strategies, and taking action to reach those goals.

It entails evaluating your existing financial status, establishing reasonable objectives, and creating plans of action to achieve them.
Making the most of your income, saving for emergencies, and planning for retirement are all made possible with financial planning.

By establishing objectives and drafting a plan of action to fulfill them, you can attain financial stability with sufficient preparation. It enables you to accumulate emergency funds to deal with unforeseen costs and shield yourself from debt.
With careful preparation, you can adequately save for retirement and ensure a comfortable future.

You may efficiently manage and minimize debt by using financial planning. It offers methods for settling credit card debt, loans, and other financial commitments.

With proper planning, you may maximize your tax liability by utilizing tax credits, deductions, and techniques to reduce your overall tax bill.

Setting priorities for your goals and drafting a strategy to achieve them are made easier with the help of financial planning. Financial planning assists you in staying on course and realizing your goals, whether they involve starting a business, purchasing a home, or paying for schooling.

Managing and reducing financial risks is a key component of financial planning since it helps you build wealth over time.

It covers strategies such as establishing emergency savings accounts, insurance, and investment diversification.

You may safeguard your loved ones against financial difficulties and yourself by being ready for unforeseen circumstances.

Above all, financial preparation eases anxiety and lessens financial strain. It helps you make wise decisions and offers you a sense of control over your finances.

Having a well-thought-out plan in place will allow you to enjoy life without having to worry about money all the time.

Budgeting

A crucial aspect of personal finance is budgeting. It entails formulating a strategy for allocating earnings and outlays.

It supports both individuals and businesses in efficiently managing their funds. People can monitor their spending, set spending priorities, and reduce their costs by using a budget. A budget lists goals for savings, expenses, and income for a given time frame, like a month or a year.

It facilitates improved financial planning and aids in the accomplishment of both immediate and long-term objectives. Effective cash flow management and debt avoidance are further benefits of budgeting.

Creating a Budget

Row Labels ▼	Sum of Spent	Planned	% of plan		Variance
Entertainment	120	200	60	✔	80
Food	251	126	200	✖	-126
Gift	200	91	220	✖	-109
Housing	94	94	100	✔	0
Personal Care	40	100	40	✔	60
Transportation	35	70	50	✔	35
Grand Total	740			✖	-60

Start by listing and calculating your total income, including wages and salaries, investments, rental income, and any other sources of income.

Next, make a list of every expense you have, including variable costs like groceries, entertainment, and travel, as well as fixed costs like utilities, rent, or mortgage payments.

Calculate your surplus or deficit by deducting your expenses from your revenue. You have extra money, a surplus, in your budget if your income is more than your outlays. On the other hand, you have a deficit if your costs are more than your revenue. In order to reach financial objectives, the aim is to minimize costs or maximize revenue.

Make sure your expenses don't exceed your income by modifying your spending patterns to meet your financial objectives.

Budgeting Tips for pre-teens and teens

- Identify your income – As a teen or preteen, you may not have a job that pays regular income. Your income may come from weekly allowance, financial gifts from relatives, or gigs such as babysitting, dog walking and lemonade sales.
- Calculate your total income
- Identify your expenses – Your required expenses may include things like your cell phone bill or your lunch at school.

- Total all your required expenses.
- Subtract your total expenses from your total income
- Do you have any leftover money? The leftover funds can be deposited into your savings account.
- You may even consider asking your parent to help you start an investment account.
- Your savings can help with bigger future purchases.
- You may also use a portion of your discretionary funds for something fun such as going to the movies.
- It's important to balance your budget. Your expenses should not exceed your income.

Different Types of Expenses

Fixed expenses: These are recurring expenses that remain the same each month, such as rent or mortgage payments, insurance premiums, and loan repayments.

Variable expenses: These expenses can fluctuate from month to month, such as groceries, entertainment, and transportation.

Discretionary expenses are non-essential expenses that you can choose to spend on, such as eating out, buying new clothes, or spending on luxury items. These expenses can be cut back or eliminated to help save money.

It's important to differentiate between needs and wants when categorizing your expenses.

Savings, Investments and Emergency Funds

Budgeting allows you to allocate a portion of your income towards savings, investments, and emergency funds.

Saving money is crucial for building an emergency fund. An emergency fund is important to allocate a portion of your budget to cover unexpected expenses. It serves as a financial security blanket in case of unfortunate events such as job loss.

As a rule, you should aim to save at least 10-20% of your income each month.

Having an emergency fund can help you avoid going into debt when faced with unexpected financial challenges.

Investing money means buying assets such as real estate, art, stocks, and bonds that appreciate in value and grow your wealth over time.

Tracking expenses

Tracking expenses helps in understanding your spending patterns and identifying areas where money can be saved. It allows for better decision-making and helps in prioritizing expenses. By tracking expenses, individuals and organizations can avoid overspending and stay within their budget.

Debt Management

Budgeting can help you manage and pay off your debts. The first step to create a debt management plan is making a list of all your debts, including credit cards, loans, and outstanding bills.
Next, allocate a portion of your budget towards debt repayment, focusing on high-interest debts first.

By budgeting and prioritizing debt repayment, you can work towards becoming debt-free and improving your financial situation.

Tracking and Adjusting Your Budget

Keeping tabs on your spending and comparing it to your budget should be a daily habit.
Utilize applications and budgeting tools to keep an eye on your expenditures and stay within your means.
As your income or expenses change, make the necessary adjustments to your budget.

To make sure your budget is in line with your financial objectives, review it from time to time.

Long-Term Financial Goals

You can better prepare for long-term financial objectives like retirement or home ownership by using a budget.
Set aside some money in your budget to save for these objectives.

To assist you in developing a strategy to reach your long-term objectives, think about speaking with a financial advisor.

Make sure you are moving closer to your objectives by reviewing and adjusting your budget on a regular basis.

Budgeting Tips

- Set realistic financial goals and prioritize them.
- Review and adjust the budget regularly to accommodate changes in income or expenses.
- Track expenses diligently using tools like budgeting apps or spreadsheets.
- Look for ways to cut back on unnecessary expenses and find ways to save money.

Common budgeting mistakes

- Underestimating expenses: Not accounting for all expenses can lead to overspending and financial stress.
- Neglecting savings: Failing to allocate money for savings can hinder progress toward financial goals.
- Not adjusting the budget: Failing to review and adjust the budget regularly can lead to inaccurate financial planning.
- Impulsive spending: Making unplanned purchases can disrupt the budget and hinder financial progress.

Budgeting apps can simplify your budgeting process and enable you to track your income and expenses in one place. They provide visual representations of your spending habits, making it easier to identify areas where you can save money. Many budgeting apps offer automatic categorization of expenses, saving you time and effort. Some apps provide personalized recommendations and tips to help you improve your financial health.

Free Budgeting Apps to simplify your budget

1. *Mint*: Offers a comprehensive overview of your finances, including budgeting, bill tracking, and credit score monitoring
2. *PocketGuard*: Focuses on helping you stay within your budget and avoid overspending

3. *YNAB* (You Need a Budget): Emphasizes proactive budgeting and provides educational resources to help you improve your financial literacy
4. *Personal Capital*: Suitable for those with investments, retirement accounts, and complex financial portfolios
5. *EveryDollar*: Created by financial expert Dave Ramsey, it follows his budgeting principles and offers a simple, zero-based budgeting approach
6. *Goodbudget:* helps you to be proactive with your budget by planning your finances rather than tracking previous spending.
7. *Empower Personal Dashboard:* is an investment tool but it also includes features helpful for individuals looking to track their spending.
8. *Honeydue: Designed to help you and your partner review and manage your finances in one place.*

Saving and Investing

Saving money entails putting money aside for unforeseen expenses or long-term objectives. Investing is the process of placing money with the goal of making a return on assets like stocks or real estate.
Achieving financial objectives and accumulating money require investing and saving. They offer financial stability and assist people in growing their assets over time.

Differentiating Saving and Investing

Saving typically involves putting money into low-risk accounts such as savings accounts or certificates of deposit (CDs), where it earns interest but may have limited growth potential.

Investing, on the other hand, involves putting money into assets like stocks, bonds, mutual funds, or real estate, which have the potential for higher returns but also come with higher risks.

Saving is more short-term focused, while investing is generally a long-term strategy for wealth accumulation.

LEARN HOW TO SET YOUR FINANCIAL GOALS THE RIGHT WAY!!

Saving allows you to build an emergency fund to cover unexpected expenses, such as medical bills or car repairs. It helps you achieve specific financial goals, such as buying a house, starting a business, or funding education.

SAVINGS *Goal*

Saving for: _____

Amount: _____

Target Date: _____

Week / Month	Goal	Actual	Remaining	Notes
Total				

101Planners.com

Saving also provides a sense of financial security and peace of mind, knowing that you have money set aside for the future.

Investing offers the potential for higher returns compared to traditional savings accounts, especially over the long term.

It helps combat inflation by allowing your money to grow at a rate that keeps up with or exceeds the rising cost of living.

Investing can provide passive income through dividends, interest, or rental income, allowing your money to work for you.

Risk and Reward

Saving is generally considered low risk, as the money is typically held in insured bank accounts. However, the returns may be lower compared to investing.

Investing involves varying degrees of risk, depending on the type of investment. Higher-risk investments may offer higher potential returns but also come with a greater chance of loss.

Balancing risk and reward are important when deciding how much to save and how much to invest.

Diversification

Diversification is a strategy that involves spreading your investments across different asset classes, industries, and geographic regions.

By diversifying, you reduce the risk of losing all your money in case one investment performs poorly.

Diversification helps to balance out the potential losses and gains, increasing the overall stability of your investment portfolio. When investing, it is critical to consider the time horizon of the investment instrument.

Time Horizon

Your time horizon refers to the length of time you have until you need to use the money you are saving or investing.

Short-term goals, such as saving for a vacation or a down payment on a house, typically have a shorter time horizon and may require more conservative investment strategies.

Long-term goals, like retirement planning, allow for a longer time horizon and may involve more aggressive investment strategies to maximize growth potential.

Tip:

Top low-cost index funds

- Vanguard Total Stock Market Index Fund (VTSMX)
- Fidelity 500 Index Fund (FXAIX)
- Schwab S&P 500 Index Fund (SWPPX)
- iShares Core S&P 500 ETF (IVV)
- Vanguard Total Bond Market Index Fund (VBMFX)
- Schwab U.S. Aggregate Bond Index Fund (SWAGX)
- iShares Core U.S. Aggregate Bond ETF (AGG)
- Vanguard Total International Stock Index Fund (VGTSX)
- Fidelity International Index Fund (FSPSX)

Factors to Consider when choosing a bank

1. Location and Accessibility
   - Consider the proximity of the bank to your home or workplace for easy access.
   - Check if the bank has multiple branches or ATMs in convenient locations.
   - Accessibility features like online banking and mobile apps can also be important.
2. Account Options and Fees
   - Look for a bank that offers the types of accounts you need, such as checking, savings, or investment accounts.
   - Compare the fees associated with each account, including monthly maintenance fees, ATM fees, and overdraft fees.
   - Some banks may offer fee waivers or lower fees for certain account features or customer profiles.
3. Services and Features
   - Consider the services and features offered by the bank, such as online banking, mobile check deposit, bill payment, and person-to-person transfers.
   - Look for additional perks like rewards programs, cashback offers, or discounts with partner merchants.
   - Evaluate the bank's customer service reputation and availability of support channels.
4. Interest Rates and APY

- Compare the interest rates offered on savings accounts, certificates of deposit (CDs), or other investment products.
- Look for banks that offer competitive Annual Percentage Yields (APY) to maximize your earnings.
- Consider whether the interest rates are fixed or variable, and if there are any requirements or limitations to earn interest.

5. Minimum Balance Requirements
   - Check if the bank has minimum balance requirements for their accounts.
   - Consider whether you can meet the minimum balance requirements consistently to avoid fees.
   - Some banks may offer options to waive the minimum balance requirements based on certain criteria.

6. Security and Fraud Protection
   - Research the bank's security measures, such as encryption protocols, multi-factor authentication, and fraud monitoring systems.
   - Look for banks that offer zero-liability policies in case of unauthorized transactions.
   - Consider if the bank provides additional security features like account alerts or credit monitoring services.

7. Reputation and Stability
   - Research the bank's reputation and stability by checking customer reviews,

ratings, and any news about the bank's financial health.
- Consider the bank's history and longevity in the industry.
- Look for banks that are insured by the Federal Deposit Insurance Corporation (FDIC) for deposit protection.
8. Additional Services
   - Consider any additional services that may be important to you, such as mortgage loans, auto loans, credit cards, or financial planning.
   - Evaluate the terms, interest rates, and fees associated with these services.
   - Look for banks that offer a comprehensive range of services to meet your financial needs.

Seek Professional Advice

Consulting with a financial advisor or planner can be advantageous as they can assist you in developing a customized savings and investment plan that takes into account your financial circumstances, risk tolerance, and objectives.

A specialist can assist you in managing the complexities of the financial markets and offer advice on asset allocation and investment selection.

Make sure the advisor you select is trustworthy, knowledgeable, and looking out for your best interest.

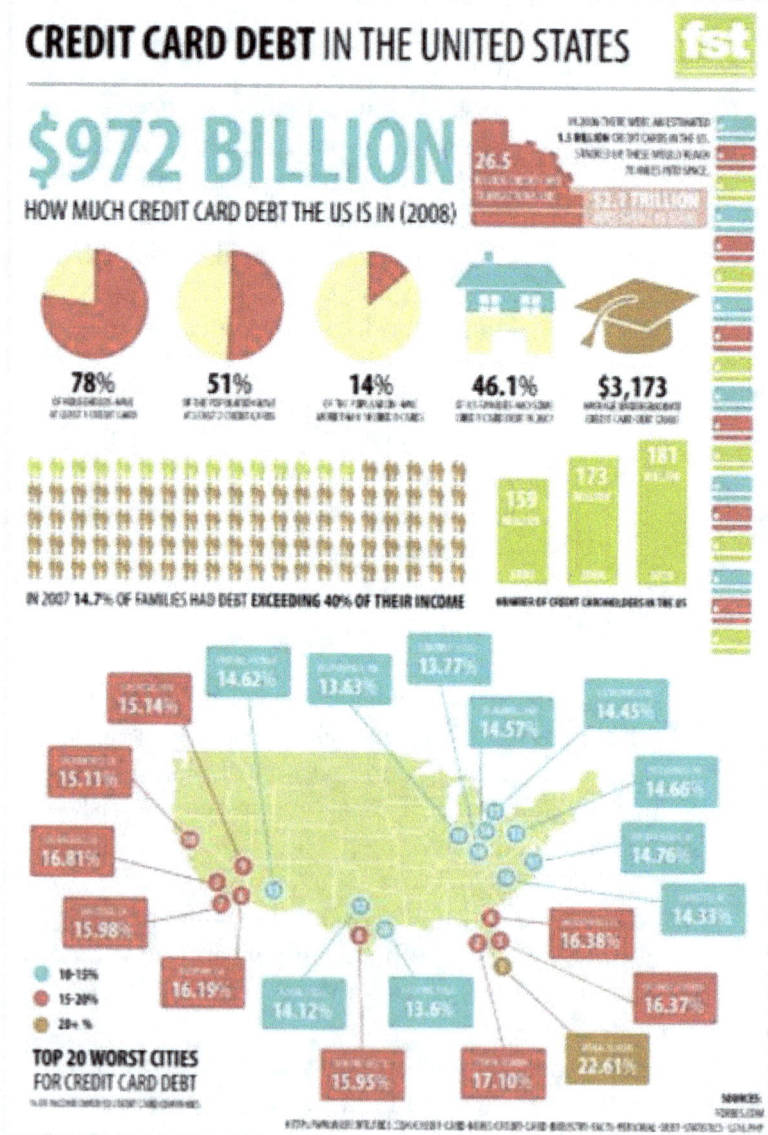

5 Ways To Dig Yourself Out Of
CREDIT CARD DEBT

1 Pay Off The Card With Highest Interest Rate
Make your *largest payment* on the card with the highest interest rate.

2 Make Minimum Payments On All Other Cards
Make the minimum payments on all the other cards *until the most expensive balance is paid off.*

3 Two Cards With The Same Interest Rate
If two cards have the same interest rate, *make a larger payment on the card with the larger balance.*

4 Maximize Your Interest Saving
Maximize your interest savings *by asking your issuers for a lower interest rate* on your credit card. A small reduction is still money saved.

5 Automating Your Payments
You might want to think about automating your payments so that you *never miss a due date* on any of your credit cards.

Bankrate.com

27

Understanding Debt and Credit

Credit is the ability to borrow money or access goods or services with the promise to pay later.

Debt is money owed to lenders or creditors.

Understanding credit and debt is crucial in personal finance to manage borrowing responsibly and avoid excessive debt.

It is important to maintain a good credit score and use credit wisely.

What is credit?

Credit is the ability to borrow money or access goods or services with the understanding that you will pay for them later.

In order to have a solid credit history—which will come in handy later on when you apply for loans or mortgages—you must first establish credit.
Credit can be acquired by loans, credit cards, or credit lines.

Types of credit

Credit comes in various forms: open credit (credit lines), installment credit (auto and school loans), and revolving credit (credit cards).
There are certain terms and restrictions associated with each sort of credit, including interest rates and repayment plans.
Prior to taking out a loan, it is critical to comprehend the terms of each form of credit.

Debt

The amount of money you owe lenders or creditors is known as your debt.

Debt can be accumulated through borrowing money, such as taking out loans or using credit cards.

Responsible debt management is essential in order to avoid financial difficulty down the road.

Good debt vs. bad debt

Good debt is debt that is used to invest in assets that

can increase in value over time, such as a mortgage for a house or a student loan for education.

Bad debt is debt that is used to purchase items that decrease in value over time, such as credit card debt for unnecessary purchases.

To keep your finances in good shape, it's critical to limit bad debt and emphasize good debt.

Credit scores

A credit score is a numerical representation of your creditworthiness, which is used by lenders to determine if you are suitable to receive financial credit based on your credit history.

Credit scores are calculated based on factors such as payment history, credit utilization, length of credit history, types of credit, and new credit.

Credit scores car range from 300 to 850.

Poor credit - 300-579

Fair credit - 580-669:

Good credit - 670-739

Very Good -740-799

Excellent Credit - 800-850

A good credit score can help you qualify for better interest rates and loan terms.

Managing credit and debt

Keeping an eye on your income and expenses will help you make sure you have enough money to pay off your debts.
Make payments on time to avoid late fees and negative impacts on your credit score.
Pay more than the minimum payment to reduce the overall amount of debt and save on interest charges.
Regularly review your credit report to check for errors and monitor your credit activity.

Tip:

Factors to Consider When Choosing a Credit Card

- Annual fees: Some credit cards charge an annual fee, while others do not. Beginners may prefer cards without annual fees to minimize costs.
- Interest rates: Look for credit cards with low-interest rates, especially if you plan to carry a balance. This can save you money on interest charges.
- Rewards and benefits: Consider the rewards and benefits offered by different credit cards,

such as cashback, travel rewards, or discounts on specific purchases.

- Credit limit: Beginners may want to start with a lower credit limit to manage their spending and avoid accumulating excessive debt.

Best Credit Cards for Beginners

- Discover it Secured: Suitable for building credit with a refundable security deposit and cashback rewards.
- Capital One Platinum Credit Card: Designed for beginners with average credit, offering credit limit increases after making on-time payments.
- Chase Freedom Unlimited: Offers cashback rewards and a 0% introductory APR for purchases.
- Citi Double Cash Card: Provides cashback rewards on all purchases, with no annual fee.
- Bank of America Cash Rewards Credit Card: Offers cashback rewards and a bonus for spending in specific categories.
- Capital One QuicksilverOne Cash Rewards Credit Card: Designed for beginners with fair credit, offering cashback rewards and credit limit increases.
- Discover it Student Cash Back: Designed for students to build credit and earn cashback rewards.
- Petal 2 "Cash Back, No Fees" Visa Credit Card: Suitable for beginners with limited

credit history, offering cashback rewards and no fees.

Credit Card Tips for Beginners

- Use your credit card for necessary expenses and emergencies, rather than impulse purchases.
- Set up automatic payments or reminders to ensure you never miss a payment.
- Regularly review your credit card statements for any unauthorized charges or errors.
- Pay your credit card bill on time and in full each month to establish a positive payment history.
- Keep your credit utilization ratio low by using only a small portion of your available credit.
- Avoid opening multiple credit cards at once, as this can negatively impact your credit score.

You can request a free copy of your credit report by visiting www.annualcreditreport.com or calling (877) 322-8228

Below is a list of credit monitoring services that can help you review your credit online:

Credit Karma - https://www.creditkarma.com/
Credit Sesame - https://www.creditsesame.com/
myFICO - https://www.myfico.com/
Experian - https://www.experian.com/
PrivacyGuard - https://www.privacyguard.com/

Identity Guard - https://www.identityguard.com/
Equifax - https://www.equifax.com/
Aura - https://www.aura.com/
IdentityForce - https://www.identityforce.com/
TransUnion - https://www.transunion.com/
LifeLock - https://lifelock.norton.com/
ID Watchdog - https://www.idwatchdog.com/

Consequences of excessive debt

Excessive debt can lead to financial stress, difficulty in obtaining future credit, and damage to your credit score.

It may limit your ability to achieve financial goals, such as buying a house or starting a business.

It is important to avoid taking on more debt than you can comfortably manage.

Strategies for debt repayment

Prioritize debt repayment by focusing on high-interest debt first.

Consider debt consolidation or balance transfer options to simplify payments and potentially reduce interest rates.

Explore strategies such as the snowball or avalanche method to systematically pay off debt. This method is used to pay off small debts as quickly as possible. Once that debt is paid off, it frees up money to tackle

the next small debt. You can continue this process
until all debts are paid off.

Insurance

Insurance is a financial product that provides
protection against potential risks and losses.

It helps individuals manage unexpected events, such
as accidents, illnesses, or property damage.

There are various kinds of insurance such as health
insurance, life insurance, auto insurance, and home
insurance.
For both peace of mind and financial stability,
insurance coverage is essential.

How insurance works

Insurance companies collect premiums from policyholders, which are used to cover potential losses.

When a covered event occurs, such as an accident or illness, the policyholder can file a claim with the insurance company. The insurance company then assesses the claim and determines the coverage and amount to be paid.

Policyholders may need to pay a deductible or co-payment before receiving the insurance benefits.

Factors affecting insurance premiums

Your age, gender, location, driving history (for vehicle insurance) and health status (for health and life insurance), as well as the kind of coverage you select and its limits and deductibles, all affect your insurance rates. The brand and model of your car, your occupation, and your credit score are some variables that may affect your premiums.

Insurance rates can be also be influenced by lifestyle decisions in addition to age and health. These factors are used by insurers to evaluate risk and determine the probability of claims.

For example, a person with a history of accidents may have higher auto insurance premiums.

Insurance companies use actuarial data and statistical models to assess risk and determine premiums.

Evaluating insurance policies

When choosing an insurance policy, it's important to compare different options and consider factors such as coverage, premiums, deductibles, and exclusions.

Reading the policy terms and conditions is crucial to understanding the coverage and limitations.

It's also advisable to assess the financial stability and reputation of the insurance company.

Insurance and financial planning

Insurance protects against unforeseen disasters, which makes it an essential component of financial planning.

It helps individuals and families maintain their financial stability and achieve long-term goals in the event of unplanned events.

Insurance can be integrated into retirement planning, ensuring a secure income stream during retirement years. (Insurance and retirement planning will be discussed in further in the retirement section)

It's important to regularly review insurance coverage to align with changing financial needs and circumstances.

Insurance fraud prevention

Insurance fraud refers to deceptive activities aimed at obtaining undeserved insurance benefits or financial gain.

It can involve false claims, staged accidents, or deliberate misrepresentation of facts.

Insurance companies have measures in place to detect and prevent fraud, including investigations and data analysis.

Policyholders should always provide accurate information and report any suspicious activities to their insurance company.

Tips to Reduce Insurance Costs

- Obtain quotes from multiple insurance providers to compare rates and coverage options
- Consider factors such as deductibles, coverage limits, and discounts offered by each provider
- Consolidate multiple insurance policies, such as auto and home insurance, with the same provider
- Bundling policies often leads to discounts and lower overall premiums
- Maintain a good credit score
- A good credit score can positively impact your insurance premiums
- Increase deductibles
- Opting for higher deductibles can lower your insurance premiums
- Evaluate your financial situation and choose a deductible that you can comfortably afford in case of a claim
- Maintain a safe driving record
- Avoid accidents and traffic violations to maintain a clean driving record
- Consider taking defensive driving courses to improve your driving skills and potentially reduce premiums

- Install safety features
- Installing safety features in your home, such as smoke detectors, burglar alarms, and fire extinguishers, can lead to insurance discounts
- Similarly, installing safety features in your vehicle, such as anti-theft devices and airbags, may result in lower auto insurance premiums
- Consult with your insurance provider to determine which safety features qualify for discounts
- Some insurance providers offer discounts or incentives for maintaining a healthy lifestyle
- Engage in regular exercise, eat a balanced diet, and avoid tobacco use to potentially qualify for these discounts
- Check with your insurance provider to see if they offer any wellness programs or incentives
- Review your coverage annually
- Contact your insurance provider to discuss any changes or updates to your policy
- Life events, such as marriage, having children, or purchasing a new home, may require adjustments to your coverage

Insurance Recap – Tips for Teens

Insurance is a financial safety net. Auto insurance is crucial when driving, to cover potential accidents and liability. Health insurance ensures access to medical care. Renters insurance protects personal belongings in a rented space. It's important for teens to know about coverage details, premiums, deductibles, and the impact of their behavior (e.g., safe driving) on insurance costs. Establishing good habits early, like maintaining a clean driving record, can lead to lower premiums in the long run.

1.   Understanding Coverage: Learn the details of your insurance policies. Understand what each type of insurance (auto, health, etc.) covers and what it doesn't.

2.   Safe Driving Habits: Developing good driving habits can not only keep you safe but also help in maintaining a clean driving record, which often translates to lower auto insurance premiums.

3.   Budgeting for Premiums: Recognize that insurance comes at a cost. Budgeting for premiums ensures that you can consistently maintain coverage without financial strain.

4.   Comparing Options: Explore and compare insurance options. Different insurers may offer varying rates and coverage, so it's essential to find a balance that suits your needs and budget.

5.   Building Credit: A good credit score can positively impact insurance premiums. Establishing responsible financial habits from a young age can contribute to lower costs.

6.   Reporting Changes: Keep your insurance provider informed of any changes in your circumstances, such as moving, getting a new car, or changes in health status. This helps ensure your

coverage remains accurate.

7.   Seeking Discounts: Inquire about available discounts. Some insurers offer discounts for good grades, completing driver's education, or bundling different types of insurance.

8.   Emergency Preparedness: Understand the procedures for making a claim. In case of an incident, knowing how to navigate the claims process is crucial for a smooth experience.

9.   Health Insurance Awareness: If you're responsible for your health insurance, understand your policy's coverage limits, copayments, and how to access healthcare services.

10.   Long-Term Perspective: Recognize that insurance is a long-term investment in your financial security. Responsible behavior now can lead to lower premiums and better coverage options in the future.

Retirement Planning

Retirement planning involves saving and investing money to ensure a comfortable retirement.

Retirement planning is crucial to ensure financial security during your retirement years. It allows you to maintain your desired lifestyle and cover expenses when you are no longer working. Starting early with retirement planning gives you more time to save and grow your funds.

It is important to start planning for retirement early to take advantage of compounding interest and maximize savings.

Retirement plans can include employer-sponsored plans like 401(k) or individual retirement accounts (IRAs). Planning for retirement helps individuals maintain their standard of living after they stop working.

Setting Retirement Goals

Determine your retirement goals, such as the age you want to retire and the lifestyle you desire.

Consider factors like healthcare costs, travel plans, and any other specific financial needs you may have.

Setting clear goals helps you create a realistic retirement plan.

Assessing Current Financial Situation

Evaluate your current financial situation, including income, expenses, and existing savings. Determine your net worth and understand your cash flow to make informed decisions.

This assessment helps you identify areas where you can save more for retirement.

Most families–even those approaching retirement–have little or no retirement savings

Median retirement account savings of families by age, 1989-2013 (2013 dollars)

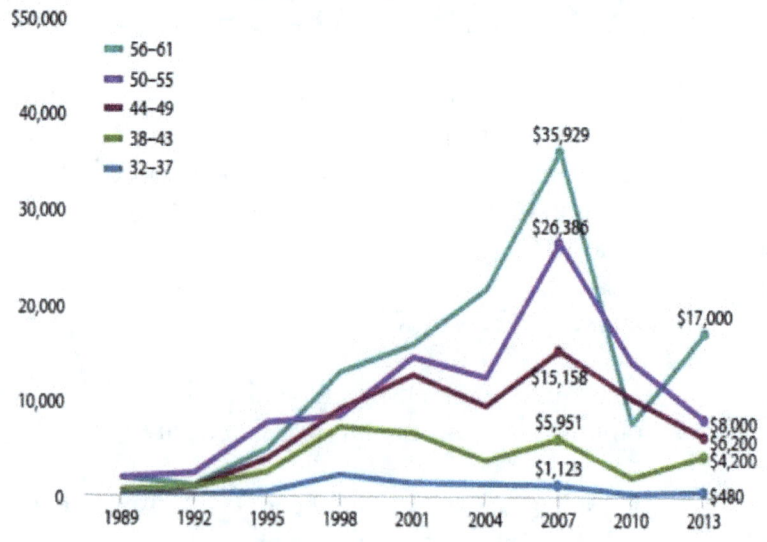

Note: Scale changed for visibility. Retirement account savings include 401(k)s, IRAs, and Keogh plans.

Source: EPI analysis of Survey of Consumer Finance data, 2013.

Retirement Savings Options

There are various types of retirement plans, including employer-sponsored plans and individual retirement accounts (IRAs).

(IRAs) are popular choices for retirement savings. IRAs are accounts that individuals can open independently, such as Traditional IRAs and Roth IRAs.

Traditional IRAs allow individuals to contribute pre-tax income, and taxes are paid when the money is withdrawn during retirement.

Roth IRAs, on the other hand, are funded with after-tax income, and withdrawals during retirement are tax-free.

Other retirement savings options, include employer-sponsored plans like 401(k) or 403(b) and pensions.

A 401(k) plan is a popular type of employer-sponsored plan where employees can contribute a portion of their salary, and employers may match a percentage of those contributions.

Contributions to a 401(k) plan are typically tax-deferred, meaning you don't pay taxes on the money until you withdraw it during retirement.

Employer Matching Contributions and Vesting Period

Some employer-sponsored retirement plans offer matching contributions.

This means that for every dollar you contribute to your retirement plan, your employer will also contribute a certain percentage, up to a specified limit.

Employer matching contributions are essentially free money that can significantly boost your retirement savings.

Some employer-sponsored retirement plans have vesting periods.

A vesting period is the length of time you must work for a company before you fully own the employer's contributions to your retirement plan. Once you are fully vested, you have complete ownership of the employer's contributions, even if you leave the company.

Some insurance policies such as whole life, universal life, or indexed universal life, can be valuable resources for people seeking future stability and financial protection in retirement. These plans offer tax benefits as well as stable income streams, which makes them appealing options for properly saving for retirement.

These particular policies accumulate funds that can be utilized for a variety of things, including debt repayment, business startup, or even retirement income through loans or withdrawal options—all while guaranteeing the protection of the policyholder and their dependents.

Tax benefits from life insurance retirement plans include growth in cash value that is tax-free until withdrawal, loans that may be exempt from interest if specific age conditions are satisfied, and, with careful preparation, death payments to beneficiaries. As long as withdrawals from these insurance are made before the policyholder's 59 1/2 birthday, they will not be taxed on the interest or investment gains made therein.

The accumulation of cash value in an insurance policy enables dependable access through loans and withdrawals, providing retirees with the assurance that there will always be money accessible when they need it. These plans can be dependable sources of financial support during retirement years because they are immune to market volatility and don't carry the hazards of stock market swings.

Retirement Plan Withdrawals
Retirement plan withdrawals can typically be made penalty-free after reaching a certain age, usually 59 ½. However, early withdrawals may incur penalties and taxes.

You should be cognizant of the rules and regulations regarding withdrawals from your retirement plan to avoid unnecessary fees.

It is crucial to understand the benefits and limitations of each option to make the best choice for your situation.

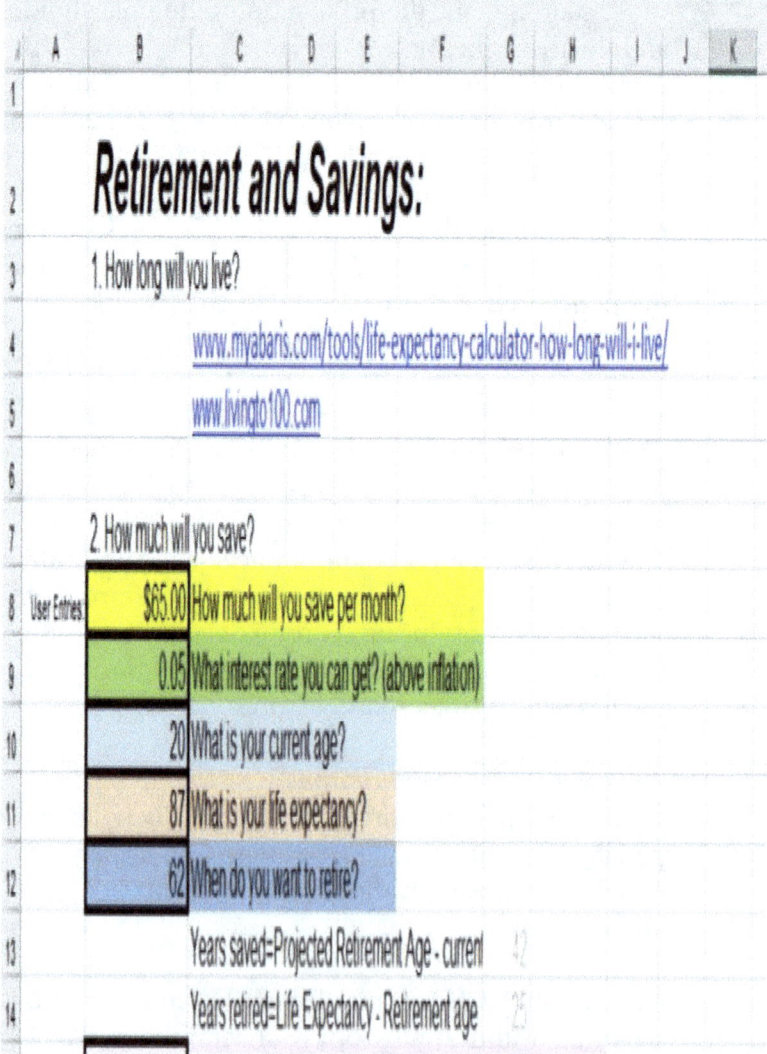

Investing for Retirement

Investing is an essential part of retirement planning to grow your savings over time.

Retirement plans offer various investment options to grow your savings over time.

Common investment options include stocks, bonds, mutual funds, and exchange-traded funds (ETFs). The choice of investments depends on your risk tolerance and financial goals.

Diversify your investments to reduce risk and maximize potential returns.

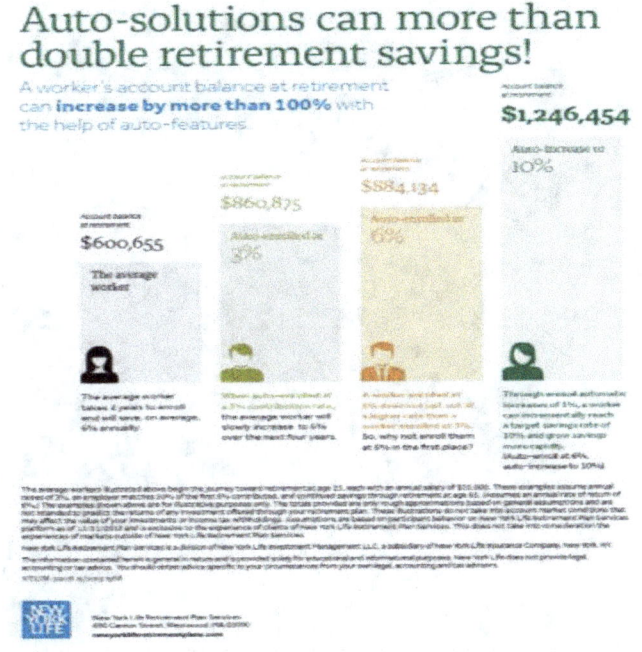

Social Security and Pension Plans

Understand how Social Security benefits work and how they can contribute to your retirement income.

If you have a pension plan through your employer, learn about its terms and conditions. These additional sources of income can supplement your retirement savings.

Managing Debt and Expenses

An important aspect of retirement planning is minimize debt and manage expenses effectively to have more disposable income for retirement savings.

Create a budget and prioritize saving for retirement as a financial goal.

If possible, prioritize paying off high-interest debts and avoid unnecessary expenses to free up funds for retirement.

Regularly review your retirement plan to ensure it aligns with your changing circumstances and goals. Adjust your contributions, investments, and savings strategies as needed.

Estate Planning

What is Estate Planning?

Estate planning is the process of arranging for the management and disposal of a person's assets after their death.

It involves creating legal documents that outline how your assets will be distributed and who will be responsible for managing them.

Estate planning is important to ensure that your wishes are carried out, minimize taxes, and provide for your loved ones.

Estate planning ensures that your assets are distributed according to your wishes, avoiding potential conflicts among family members.

It allows you to minimize estate taxes and other expenses, preserving more of your wealth for your loved ones.

Estate planning also includes provisions for incapacity, ensuring that someone you trust can make decisions on your behalf if you become unable to do so.

Key Components of Estate Planning

Will: A legal document that specifies how your assets will be distributed after your death.

Trust: A legal arrangement where a trustee holds and manages assets on behalf of beneficiaries.

Power of Attorney: A legal document that grants someone the authority to make financial decisions on your behalf if you become incapacitated.

Healthcare Proxy: A legal document that designates someone to make medical decisions for you if you are unable to do so.

Estate Planning Process

1. Gather information about your assets, debts, and beneficiaries.

2. Consult with an estate planning attorney to discuss your goals and create the necessary legal documents.
3. Review and update your estate plan regularly to reflect any changes in your circumstances or wishes.

Types of Estate Planning Documents

Last Will and Testament: Specifies how your assets will be distributed after your death.

Living Trust: Allows you to transfer assets to a trust during your lifetime, avoiding probate.

Advance Healthcare Directive: Outlines your medical treatment preferences and designates a healthcare proxy.

Financial Power of Attorney: Grants someone the authority to make financial decisions on your behalf.

Probate and Estate Administration

Probate is the legal process of administering a deceased person's estate, including validating the will, paying debts, and distributing assets.

Proper estate planning can help minimize the time and costs associated with probate.

Estate administration involves the management and distribution of assets according to the terms of the estate plan.

Estate Taxes

Estate taxes are taxes imposed on the transfer of property after death.

Proper estate planning can help minimize estate taxes through strategies such as gifting, trusts, and charitable donations.

Estate tax laws vary by jurisdiction, so it's important to consult with an estate planning attorney to understand the specific rules that apply to you.

Choosing an Estate Planning Attorney

An estate planning attorney specializes in creating and implementing estate plans.

When choosing an attorney, consider their experience, expertise, and reputation.

It's important to work with an attorney who understands your goals and can help you navigate the complexities of estate planning.

Taxes

Taxes are compulsory financial contributions imposed by the government on individuals and businesses.

Understanding taxes is important in personal finance to comply with tax laws and avoid penalties.

Different types of taxes include income tax, sales tax, and property tax.

Types of taxes

The most common type of tax is income tax, which is a percentage of your earnings that you must pay to the government. If you earn income of any kind, you must file tax returns accurately. Filing your tax returns will not only put you in compliance with the Internal Revenue Service (IRS) laws, it also allows you take advantage of available deductions and credits outlined in the tax codes.

Other types of taxes include sales tax, property tax, and excise tax.

Each type of tax has its own rules and regulations, and the rates may vary depending on your income level and location.

How are taxes calculated?

Taxes are calculated based on your taxable income, which is the amount of income you have after deductions and exemptions.

The tax rate you pay depends on your income level and tax bracket.

The government provides tax forms and online tools to help you calculate your taxes accurately.

Deductions and exemptions

Deductions and exemptions are ways to reduce your taxable income and lower your tax liability.

Common deductions include mortgage interest, student loan interest, and charitable contributions.

Exemptions are allowances for certain expenses, such as medical expenses or dependents.

Filing your taxes

To file your taxes, you need to gather all relevant financial documents, such as W-2 forms, 1099 forms, and receipts. The deadline to file your taxes is usually April 15th, but it may vary depending on the year and your location.

Tax credits

Tax credits are incentives provided by the government to encourage certain behaviors or support specific groups.

Examples of tax credits include the child tax credit, education credits, and renewable energy credits.

Tax credits directly reduce your tax liability, so they can result in significant savings.ax

Taxes Recap Tips for Teens

1.   Understanding Income: Know the difference between earned income (from jobs) and unearned income (interest, dividends).

2.   Filing Requirement: Understand when you need to file a tax return. Typically, it depends on your income level and filing status.

3.   Forms and Deadlines: Familiarize yourself with common tax forms like W-2 and 1099. Be aware of tax deadlines and the importance of filing on time. A W-2 shows income earned from your

employer, taxes withheld and other employer benefits you received for a specific tax year. A 1099 is used to report non-employee income to the IRS.

4.   Taxable vs. Non-taxable Income: Learn what types of income are taxable and which are not. Scholarships, for example, might be nontaxable if used for qualified education expenses.

5.   Deductions and Credits: Know the difference between deductions (reduce taxable income) and credits (directly reduce taxes owed). Education credits, like the American Opportunity Credit, might be relevant.

6.   Understanding Withholding: Comprehend the concept of withholding taxes from your paycheck and how it impacts your tax liability. Withholding tax is the money that an employer deducts from an employee's gross wages and pays directly to the government.

7.   Bank Accounts and Taxes: Be aware of interest earned on bank accounts; it is considered taxable income.

8.   Tax Filing Software: Familiarize yourself with online tax filing tools. Many are user-friendly and can guide you through the process, especially for simpler tax situations.

9.   Dependency Status: Understand the criteria for being claimed as a dependent on someone else's tax return.

10. Financial Literacy: Develop a basic understanding of financial literacy, as it will help you make informed decisions about saving, investing, and managing your finances, which can impact your taxes.

Entrepreneurship

Introduction to Entrepreneurship

Entrepreneurship is the process of starting and running a business venture. Entrepreneurs are individuals who identify opportunities and take risks to create innovative solutions. They are driven by a desire for independence, financial success, and making a positive impact.

Problem	Solution	Unique Value Proposition	Community Relationships	Users
What problem are you trying to solve for your users? Open source considerations Why is the solution open source? • To provide free offering? • To build up community? • Other reasons?	What is the solution? Open source considerations Independent versus Foundation? Which License?	What is the promise of your project? Open source considerations Does the fact that it is open source contribute to the uniqueness of your offering? How?	What are strategic relationships that are critical to building up your community? • Contributors • Project evangelists • Thought leaders • Integrations with other projects	Describe a typical user of your project Contributors Who are users that are most likely to contribute to your project – Super Users?
	Activities What are the inbound and outbound activities you will carry out to encourage engagement with the project (e.g. conferences, blog posts, social media etc.)?		**Channels** Through which channels will you reach your users? • Collaboration partners who will distribute/expose project • Web, Social media etc. • Face to face (meetups, conferences etc.)	

Cost and Resources	Adoption Criteria
What human resources are required? Examples. • Project Maintainers (responsible for code governance etc.) • Paid engineers (core team to initiate the project or continue contributing) • Community Manager • Evangelist • Contributors to Community (not paid) Other costs? Examples: • Infrastructure/services • marketing	How do you measure success of the project? Examples. • Size of community (number of issues/pull requests/stars etc.) • Number of contributors • Contributions (scale, variety, etc.) • Usage • Conversion rate (if your business model includes upgrade to enterprise version)

Open Source Canvas is adapted from the Business Model Canvas and the Lean Canvas and is licensed under Attribution-ShareAlike 4.0 International

Characteristics of successful entrepreneurs:

Successful entrepreneurs possess qualities such as creativity, resilience, determination, and a willingness to learn.

They are proactive and take initiative, constantly seeking new opportunities

They are adaptable and able to navigate challenges and setbacks

Steps to starting a business

1. Identify a business idea or opportunity
2. Conduct market research to assess demand and competition
3. Develop a business plan outlining the company's goals, strategies, and financial projections
4. Secure funding and resources
5. Register the business and comply with legal requirements.

Risks and rewards of entrepreneurship

Entrepreneurship involves risks such as financial uncertainty, long working hours, and the possibility of failure. However, successful entrepreneurs can enjoy financial independence, personal fulfillment, and the satisfaction of creating something meaningful. The potential rewards outweigh the risks for many individuals.

Types of entrepreneurship

Traditional entrepreneurship focuses on creating profitable businesses.

Social entrepreneurship aims to address social or environmental issues while generating revenue. Intrapreneurship refers to entrepreneurial activities within existing organizations

Skills needed for entrepreneurship

Communication and networking skills to build relationships and attract customers.

Financial management skills to handle budgets, cash flow, and investments.

Marketing and sales skills to promote products or services.

Leadership and team-building skills to manage employees and collaborators

Resources for aspiring entrepreneurs

Business incubators and accelerators provide mentorship, resources, and funding to startups. Entrepreneurship education programs offer courses and workshops on business fundamentals and skills. Online platforms and communities connect entrepreneurs for knowledge sharing and support.

Tips and Tricks to Build Wealth

Getting Started with Investments

- Before you start investing, it's important to have clear financial goals in mind.
- Determine what you want to achieve with your investments, such as saving for retirement, buying a house, or funding your children's education.
- Understand Risk and Return
- Generally, higher-risk investments have the potential for higher returns, while lower-risk investments offer more stability but lower returns.
- Diversifying your portfolio across different asset classes can help manage risk and optimize returns.
- Before diving into complex investment options, build a solid financial foundation.
- Establish an emergency fund to cover unexpected expenses.
- Pay off high-interest debt, such as credit card balances, to reduce financial stress.
- Create a budget and manage your expenses effectively to free up money for investments.
- For beginners, a good starting point is investing in low-cost index funds.
- Index funds are designed to track specific market indexes, such as the S&P 500.

- Invest Regularly and Consistently. Consistency is key when it comes to investing.
- Set up automatic contributions to your investment accounts on a regular basis.
- Avoid trying to time the market and focus on long-term investing.

Tips for reducing rental costs

- Consider living in a less expensive area or neighborhood.
- Research the rental prices in different locations to find the most affordable option.
- Look for areas with lower demand or upcoming developments that may offer lower rent prices.
- Consider sharing a rental space with roommates to split the cost.
- Negotiate with the landlord or property manager for a lower rent price.
- Highlight your good rental history, stable income, or any other factors that may make you an attractive tenant.
- Opt for a longer lease term, such as a year, to negotiate a lower monthly rent.
- Landlords may be more willing to reduce the rent for tenants who commit to a longer stay.
- Look for rental opportunities during off-peak seasons when demand is lower.
- Landlords may offer discounted rates or incentives to fill vacant units.

- Be flexible with your move-in date to take advantage of these opportunities.
- Choose rental properties with include utilities or amenities to save on additional expenses.
- Consider energy-efficient options to reduce utility costs, such as LED light bulbs or smart thermostats.
- Prioritize your needs and evaluate the value of included amenities before making a decision.
- Rental Assistance Programs.
- Research and inquire about rental assistance programs offered by local or government organizations.
- These programs may provide financial aid or subsidies to eligible individuals or families.
- Check the eligibility criteria and application process to determine if you qualify for assistance.

To Rent or to Buy? That is the question.

Advantages of Renting

- Flexibility: Renting allows you to easily move to a new location or upgrade to a bigger space without the hassle of selling a property.
- Lower upfront costs: Renting typically requires a smaller upfront payment compared to buying a house, as you only need to pay a security deposit and possibly the first month's rent.

- Maintenance and repairs: When you rent, the responsibility for maintenance and repairs usually falls on the landlord, saving you time and money.

Advantages of Buying

- Equity and investment: Buying a property allows you to build equity over time, which can be a valuable asset. Additionally, if the property appreciates in value, you may make a profit when you sell it.
- Freedom to customize: As a homeowner, you have the freedom to personalize and modify your living space according to your preferences.
- Stability: Owning a home provides a sense of stability and security, as you don't have to worry about rent increases or the possibility of being asked to leave.

Disadvantages of Renting

- No equity: When you rent, you do not build equity in the property, meaning you won't benefit from any potential increase in its value.
- Limited control: Renting restricts your ability to make major changes to the property, as you need permission from the landlord.
- Rent increases: Landlords can increase rent periodically, potentially making it more

expensive to continue living in the same place.

Disadvantages of Buying

- Financial commitment: Buying a house requires a significant financial commitment, including a down payment, mortgage payments, property taxes, and maintenance costs.
- Limited flexibility: Selling a property can be a lengthy and complex process, limiting your ability to quickly relocate or downsize.
- Responsibility for maintenance: As a homeowner, you are responsible for the maintenance and repairs of the property, which can be costly and time-consuming.

How to avoid unnecessary Debt.

- Create a Budget
- Track your income and expenses to understand your financial situation
- Prioritize essential expenses and limit discretionary spending
- Build an emergency fund to cover unexpected expenses
- Start saving for retirement early to take advantage of compounding interest
- Investing in low-cost index funds for long-term growth
- Avoid unnecessary debt by saving up for major purchases instead of relying on credit

- Manage Credit Wisely
- Pay your bills on time to avoid late fees and negative marks on your credit report
- Keep your credit utilization ratio low by using only a small portion of your available credit
- Regularly check your credit report for errors and dispute any inaccuracies
- Minimize Student Loans
- Research and apply for scholarships and grants to reduce the need for loans
- Consider attending a community college or trade school before transferring to a four-year university
- Borrow only what you absolutely need for tuition and living expenses
- Explore income-driven repayment plans and loan forgiveness options after graduation
- Avoid Impulse Buying
- Make a shopping list and stick to it to avoid unnecessary purchases
- Wait 24 hours before making a non-essential purchase to avoid impulse buying
- Build an Emergency Fund
- Aim to save three to six months' worth of living expenses in case of emergencies
- Start small by setting aside a portion of your income each month
- Automate your savings by setting up automatic transfers to a separate savings account
- Use your emergency fund only for true emergencies, not for discretionary spending

- Live Within Your Means
- Differentiate between needs and wants to prioritize essential expenses
- Avoid lifestyle inflation and resist the urge to spend more as your income increases

Tips to save on shopping.

- Create a shopping list before heading to the store to avoid impulse purchases and stay focused on what you need.

- Organize the list by priority, placing essential items at the top and non-essential items at the bottom.
- Research prices online or use price comparison apps to find the best deals on the items you need.
- Check multiple stores or websites to ensure you are getting the lowest price.
- Consider factors like shipping costs and return policies when comparing prices.
- Use Coupons and Discounts
- Look for coupons in newspapers, magazines, or online coupon websites.
- Sign up for store loyalty programs to receive exclusive discounts and rewards.
- Take advantage of seasonal sales, clearance racks, and promotional offers to save money.
- Keep an eye out for sales events like Black Friday, Cyber Monday, or end-of-season sales.

- Consider purchasing generic or store-brand products instead of name brands.

Tips on financing your education

- Scholarships and Grants - Scholarships and grants are free money that you don't have to pay back.
- Federal Student Aid -The Free Application for Federal Student Aid (FAFSA) is a form that determines your eligibility for federal financial aid programs.
- Work-Study Programs - Work-study programs provide part-time employment opportunities for students to earn money while in college
- Savings and Budgeting - Start saving for college as early as possible to reduce the amount you need to borrow.
- Part-Time Jobs - Getting a part-time job while in college can help cover living expenses and reduce reliance on loans.
- Student loans are borrowed money that must be repaid with interest. Before taking out loans, exhaust all other options for financial aid, such as scholarships, grants, and work-study programs.
- Parental Support - Talk to your parents or guardians about their ability to contribute to your college expenses.
- Explore alternative funding sources such as crowdfunding platforms, community organizations, or employer tuition assistance programs.

- Some colleges and universities offer payment plans that allow you to spread out the cost of tuition over several months.
- Research and apply for private scholarships and grants from organizations or foundations related to your field of study.

Reward Yourself

It takes personal discipline to create financial health and build wealth. A big part of the journey involves practicing delayed gratification. That is not always easy to do. I believe it is important to reward yourself along the way to financial wellness. After all, if you are going to delay gratification and not go on that shopping spree, at least plan to reward yourself when you reach milestones.

Rewarding yourself is an essential part of financial success as it helps to maintain motivation and satisfaction.

Tips on rewarding yourself.

Plan for special purchases or splurges that you want to reward yourself with. Incorporate rewards into your budgeting plan to ensure they are affordable and won't jeopardize your financial stability.

Set aside a specific amount of money each month towards these splurges. This way, you can enjoy them guilt-free without impacting your overall financial goals. When allocating specific portions of

70

your income towards rewarding yourself, keep in mind your long-term financial goals.

Celebrate reaching financial milestones, such as paying off a debt or achieving a savings goal. Treat yourself to a small reward when you reach a savings goal or pay off a debt. This will help you stay motivated and reinforce positive financial habits. Celebrating milestones and achievements can boost your self-esteem and provide a sense of accomplishment.

Share your success with loved ones by organizing a small gathering or outing to commemorate your achievements. Surrounding yourself with supportive people can enhance the joy of celebrating your financial milestones.

Consider indulging in a small luxury item, going on a vacation, or enjoying a nice meal at your favorite restaurant.

It's important to choose rewards that align with your values and bring you joy without derailing your financial progress.

Acknowledging your hard work and dedication by treating yourself and enjoying the fruits of your labor is a vital part of the journey to financial wellness.

Non-Monetary Rewards

Remember that rewards don't always have to involve spending money.

Treat yourself to self-care activities at home like a spa day, a relaxing bath, or a day dedicated to your hobbies.

Taking care of your mental and physical well-being is an important aspect of rewarding yourself for financial success.

Long-Term Rewards

Consider long-term rewards that align with your financial goals, such as investing in your education or retirement savings.

By prioritizing long-term rewards, you are setting yourself up for sustained financial well-being.

Striking a balance between rewarding yourself and maintaining financial discipline is crucial.

Ensure that your rewards do not compromise your progress toward your financial goals.

Regularly reassess your rewards system to ensure it aligns with your evolving financial situation and priorities.

Charitable Giving

Charitable giving refers to the act of donating money, goods, or services to organizations or individuals in need. It is a way to support causes and make a positive impact on society.

Charitable giving can take various forms, such as donating money, volunteering time, or giving away possessions.

Benefits of Charitable Giving

Charitable giving provides a sense of fulfillment and satisfaction by helping others in need.

It can create a positive impact on the community and contribute to social change.

Charitable giving can also have personal benefits, such as tax deductions and increased happiness and well-being.

Types of Charitable Organizations

Charitable organizations can be classified into different categories, including health-related organizations, educational institutions, environmental groups, and social welfare organizations.

Each type of organization focuses on addressing specific needs and issues in society.

Examples of charitable organizations include the Red Cross, UNICEF, local food banks, and animal shelters.

Ways to Give

There are various ways to give charitably, such as

making monetary donations online, through check or cash, or setting up recurring donations.

Volunteering time and skills to charitable organizations is another way to contribute.

Donating goods or services, such as clothing, food, or professional expertise, is also a form of charitable giving.

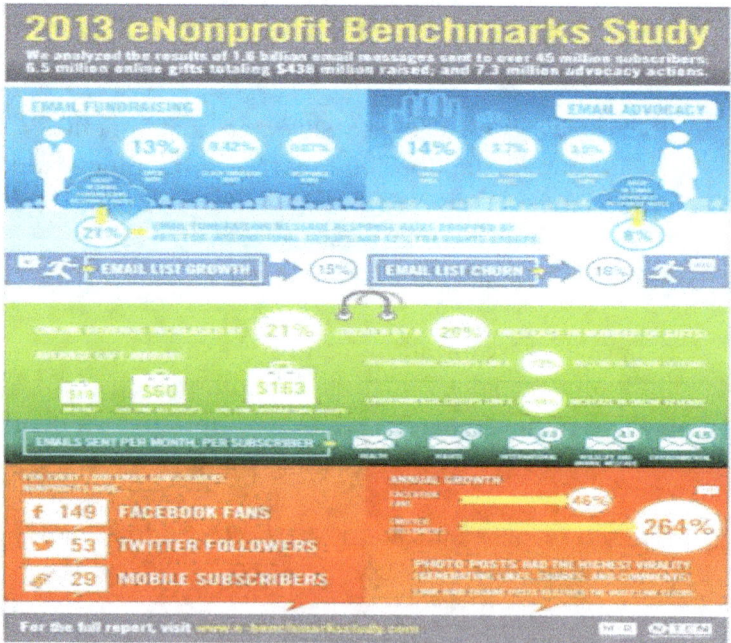

Before donating to a charitable organization, it is important to research and ensure its credibility and transparency.

Look for organizations that have a clear mission, financial accountability, and a track record of making a positive impact.

Websites like Charity Navigator and GuideStar provide information and ratings on various charitable organizations.

Tax Benefits of Charitable Giving

Charitable giving can have tax benefits, as donations to eligible organizations are tax-deductible.

Keep track of donations and obtain receipts or acknowledgment letters from the organizations to claim deductions.

Charitable giving can have a significant impact on individuals, communities, and society as a whole.

It can provide essential resources and support to those in need, such as food, shelter, education, and healthcare.

Charitable giving also contributes to research, advocacy, and initiatives aimed at addressing social issues and creating positive change.

When deciding on charitable giving, consider causes that align with your values and interests.

Assess your financial capacity and set a budget for charitable contributions.

It is also important to evaluate the effectiveness and efficiency of organizations in utilizing donations to make a meaningful impact.

Protect Your Information

Prevent Identity Theft

A critical part of your personal finance journey is safeguarding your personal information from identity theft. The potential harm from identity theft can be far-reaching and could destroy all your monetary and economic accomplishments.

Identity theft is when someone steals your personal information and uses it without your permission, often for financial gain. It can happen through various means, such as hacking into your online accounts, stealing your mail, or even posing as someone else to gain access to your personal information.

Identity theft can have serious consequences, including financial loss, damage to your credit score, and even legal issues.

Common Identity Theft Scams

Phishing scams involve fraudulent emails, text messages, or phone calls that trick individuals into revealing their personal information or login credentials.

Fake websites, often designed to look like legitimate ones, are used to collect sensitive information from unsuspecting victims.

Other common identity theft scams include fake job offers, lottery scams, and fake charity requests.

Being cautious and skeptical of unsolicited requests for personal information can help prevent falling victim to these scams.

How to protect your personal information

Be cautious when sharing personal information online, especially on social media platforms. Limit the amount of personal information you share publicly.

Use strong and unique passwords for all your online accounts, and consider using a password manager to keep track of them.

Be wary of phishing attempts, where scammers try to trick you into revealing your personal information through fraudulent emails or websites.

Regularly review your financial statements and credit reports to detect any suspicious activity.

Credit monitoring services can help individuals keep track of their credit history and detect any suspicious activity or unauthorized accounts.

Regularly reviewing credit reports from major credit bureaus allows individuals to identify any errors or signs of identity theft.

Reporting any suspicious activity or identity theft incidents to the appropriate authorities, such as the Federal Trade Commission (FTC), is essential. Taking prompt action can help minimize the damage caused by identity theft.

Securing your devices

Keep your devices, such as smartphones, laptops, and tablets, locked with a passcode or biometric authentication.

Install and regularly update security software, such as antivirus and anti-malware programs, on all your devices.

Avoid connecting to public Wi-Fi networks, as they can be insecure and allow hackers to intercept your data.

Enable two-factor authentication whenever possible to add an extra layer of security to your accounts.

Safeguarding your mail

Retrieve your mail promptly and consider using a locked mailbox or a post office box to prevent mail theft.

Shred any documents containing sensitive information, such as bank statements or credit card offers, before disposing of them.

Opt for electronic statements and bills whenever possible to reduce the amount of personal information sent through the mail.

Being cautious with phone calls and emails

Be skeptical of unsolicited phone calls or emails asking for personal information, even if they seem legitimate.

Do not provide personal information over the phone or through email unless you initiated the contact and are certain of the recipient's identity.

Be cautious of clicking on links or downloading attachments from unknown or suspicious sources, as they may contain malware or phishing attempts.

Monitoring your credit and accounts

Regularly monitor your credit reports from the major credit bureaus to detect any unauthorized activity.

Consider placing a fraud alert or credit freeze on your credit reports to prevent identity thieves from opening new accounts in your name.

Keep a close eye on your bank and credit card statements for any suspicious transactions and report them immediately.

Protecting your social security number

Avoid carrying your social security card in your wallet or purse unless absolutely necessary.

Be cautious when providing your social security number, and only share it with trusted entities that have a legitimate need for it.

Regularly check your social security earnings statement to ensure there are no discrepancies or signs of fraudulent activity.

Staying informed and proactive

Stay updated on the latest identity theft trends and scams by following reputable sources of cybersecurity news.

Educate yourself about common identity theft techniques and learn how to recognize and avoid them.

Be proactive in protecting your personal information and take immediate action if you suspect any signs of identity theft.

Ten Takeaways for Financial Management

1. **Track Your Expenses** - Start by tracking all your expenses, including small purchases and recurring bills
2. **Automate Your Savings** - Set up automatic transfers from your checking account to a savings account
3. **Reduce Unnecessary Expenses** - Review your monthly expenses and identify items that are not essential
4. **Negotiate Bills and Fees** - Contact your service providers to negotiate better rates for your bills, reduce interest rates on loans or credit cards
5. **Earn Extra Income** - Consider taking on a side gig or freelancing to increase your income
6. **Practice Mindful Spending** - Before making a purchase, ask yourself if it aligns with your financial goals
7. **Invest Wisely** - Educate yourself about different investment options such as stocks, bonds, or mutual funds and diversify your portfolio.
8. **Prioritize Debt Repayment** - Consider debt consolidation, negotiate lower interest rates, make consistent payments, and avoid accumulating more debt.
9. **Retain an accountability partner** or financial advisor to help you stay motivated and on track
10. REWARD YOURSELF AND ENJOY THE JOURNEY

Quiz

What is the purpose of taxes?

    a. Taxes are mandatory payments to fund public services and programs.
    b. Taxes are optional contributions to support local communities.
    c. Taxes are voluntary payments to fund personal expenses and investments.

Which type of tax is calculated based on your earnings?

    a. Sales tax
    b. Income tax
    c. Property tax
    d. Excise tax

How are taxes calculated?

    a. Taxes are calculated based on taxable income and tax rates.
    b. Taxes are calculated based on the number of dependents and exemptions.
    c. Taxes are calculated based on the total amount of expenses and deductions.

What are deductions and exemptions used for?

    a. Deductions and exemptions are additional taxes imposed on high-income earners.
    b. Deductions and exemptions are used to calculate tax credits and rebates.

c. Deductions and exemptions reduce taxable income and tax liability.

What does insurance provide?

a. Financial protection against potential losses or damages
b. Legal advice and representation in case of accidents
c. Investment opportunities for long-term financial growth
d. Assistance with tax planning and preparation

Which type of insurance covers medical expenses?

a. Home insurance
b. Life insurance
c. Health insurance

What is the purpose of insurance?

a. Generate additional income through investment returns
b. Mitigate financial risks and provide peace of mind
c. Guarantee employment opportunities in the insurance industry

How do insurance companies determine coverage and payment amounts?

a. Randomly selecting a predetermined amount to be paid

b. Calculating the coverage based on the insurance company's profits
c. Consulting with the policyholder's friends and family for input
d. Assessing the claim filed by the policyholder

What factors can influence insurance premiums?

a. The policyholder's favorite color and food preferences.
b. The number of social media followers the policyholder has
c. The distance between the policyholder's home and the nearest park
d. Type of insurance, coverage limits, deductibles, and risk profile.

What is the main purpose of retirement planning?

a. To maximize current income and expenses
b. To invest in high-risk ventures for quick returns
c. To ensure financial security during retirement years
d. To pay off all debts and become financially independent

Why is it beneficial to start retirement planning early?

a. It provides more time to save and grow funds
b. It allows for early retirement at a younger age
c. It guarantees a higher return on investment

d. It reduces the need for financial assessment

What should be considered when setting retirement goals?

   a. Current income and expenses only
   b. The availability of social security benefits
   c. Factors like healthcare costs, travel plans, and specific financial needs

What is an important step in assessing the current financial situation for retirement planning?

   a. Focusing solely on net worth and cash flow
   b. Evaluating income, expenses, and existing savings
   c. Focusing solely on net worth and cash flow
   d. Ignoring the importance of setting retirement goals

What are some popular retirement savings options?

   a. Real estate investments and cryptocurrency
   b. Personal savings accounts and high-yield bonds
   c. Social security benefits and pension plans
   d. Employer-sponsored plans like 401(k) or 403(b) and Individual Retirement Accounts (IRAs)

What is credit?

   a. Credit is the act of repaying borrowed money immediately.

b. Credit is the process of saving money for future expenses.

c. Credit is the ability to borrow money or access goods or services with the understanding that you will pay for them later.

d. Credit is the act of investing money in stocks and bonds.

What is a credit score?

a. A credit score is a numerical representation of your income level.

b. A credit score is a numerical representation of your debt amount.

c. A credit score is a numerical representation of your creditworthiness, which is used by lenders to determine your creditworthiness.

What is good debt?

a. Good debt is debt that is used to purchase luxury items and experiences.

b. Good debt is debt that is used to invest in assets that can increase in value over time, such as a mortgage for a house or a student loan for education.

c. Good debt is debt that is used to pay off existing debts.

d. Good debt is debt that is used to fund vacations and travel.

How can you manage credit and debt effectively?

    a. Make only the minimum payments to reduce the overall amount of debt.
    b. Regularly review your credit report to check for errors and monitor your credit activity.
    c. Avoid creating a budget to track your income and expenses.
    d. Ignore your credit report and credit score as they are not important.

What is the main difference between saving and investing?

    a. Saving involves setting aside a portion of your income, while investing involves putting money into assets.
    b. Saving is a short-term strategy, while investing is a long-term strategy.
    c. Saving has higher potential returns, while investing has lower potential returns.
    d. Saving is riskier than investing due to market fluctuations.

Why is saving important?

    a. Saving is only necessary for short-term financial needs.
    b. Saving allows you to build an emergency fund and achieve financial goals.
    c. Saving guarantees high returns on your money.
    d. Saving helps you generate passive income.

What is the purpose of diversification in investing?

    a. Diversification reduces the risk of losing all your money in case one investment performs poorly

    b. Diversification guarantees high returns on your investments.

    c. Diversification increases the potential for losses in your investment portfolio.

    d. Diversification is only necessary for short-term investment goals.

What is the purpose of budgeting?

    a. To increase spending and live beyond your means.

    b. To track income and expenses and prioritize financial goals.

    c. To avoid saving money and accumulate debt.

    d. To randomly allocate money without any financial goals.

How can budgeting help with debt management?

    a. By allocating a portion of the budget towards debt repayment.

    b. By ignoring debt and focusing solely on savings.

    c. By spending more money and accumulating more debt.

    d. By avoiding budgeting altogether and hoping debt will disappear.

What are fixed expenses?

    a. Expenses that vary from month to month.
    b. Non-essential expenses that can be easily cut.
    c. Recurring costs that remain the same each month.

Why is it important to differentiate between needs and wants when categorizing expenses?

    a. To randomly categorize expenses without any distinction.
    b. To eliminate all wants and focus solely on needs.
    c. To spend all income on wants and ignore needs.
    d. To prioritize essential expenses and avoid overspending.

How can budgeting help with long-term financial goals?

    a. By allocating a portion of the budget towards saving for those goals.
    b. By spending all income on short-term desires.
    c. By ignoring long-term goals and focusing on immediate gratification.
    d. By relying solely on luck and chance to achieve long-term goals.

What is one advantage of renting a property?

    a. Flexibility
    b. Lower upfront costs
    c. Equity and investment
    d. Freedom to customize

What is one advantage of buying a property?

a. Rent increases
b. Equity and investment
c. Limited control
d. No equity
e. What is one disadvantage of renting a property?

What is one disadvantage of renting a property?

a. Financial commitment
b. Limited control
c. Flexibility

What is one disadvantage of buying a property?

a. Limited flexibility
b. No equity
c. Rent increases
d. Lower upfront costs

How can you protect your personal information online?

    a. Be cautious when sharing personal information online, especially on social

media platforms. Limit the amount of personal information you share publicly.
   b. Use the same password for all your online accounts for convenience.
   c. Share personal information freely on all online platforms to build trust.
   d. Ignore any suspicious emails or messages asking for personal information.

What is the purpose of estate planning?

   a. To minimize estate taxes and other expenses.
   b. To ensure assets are distributed according to your wishes.
   c. To appoint a healthcare proxy for medical decisions.
   d. To create legal documents for managing and disposing of assets

Which document allows you to transfer assets to a trust during your lifetime?

   a. Living Trust
   b. Last Will and Testament
   c. Advance Healthcare Directive
   d. Financial Power of Attorney

How can estate planning help minimize taxes?

   a. By creating legal documents for managing and disposing of assets
   b. By transferring assets to a trust during your lifetime

c. By appointing a healthcare proxy for medical decisions

d. Through strategies such as gifting, trusts, and charitable donations

What is entrepreneurship?

a. Entrepreneurship is the act of investing in established companies

b. Entrepreneurship is the process of starting and running a business venture

c. Entrepreneurship is the art of managing personal finances effectively

d. Entrepreneurship is the practice of working as an employee in a business

What are the risks and rewards of entrepreneurship?

a. Entrepreneurship guarantees financial stability and a balanced work-life schedule.

b. Entrepreneurship involves risks such as financial uncertainty, long working hours, and the possibility of failure.

c. Entrepreneurship eliminates all risks and guarantees immediate success.

d. Entrepreneurship offers no rewards and is not worth pursuing.

What is the definition of charitable giving?

a. Engaging in activities that contribute to social change.

b. Supporting causes and making a positive impact on society.

c. Volunteering time and skills to charitable organizations.
d. Donating money, goods, or services to organizations or individuals in need.

How can charitable giving benefit individuals?

a. It provides a sense of fulfillment and satisfaction.
b. It offers tax deductions and financial benefits.
c. It increases happiness and well-being.
d. It creates opportunities for personal growth and development.

www.ingramcontent.com/pod-product-compliance
Lightning Source LLC
Chambersburg PA
CBHW071057290526
45795CB00004B/1541